The Infernal Now

For Jim & Lois,
with affection and
admiration,
Anne

2022

The Infernal Now

Poems by

Arnold Johnston

Cover by Shay Culligan
Cover image by Peter Gooch, *Fan of the Baroque Madonna*

ISBN: 978-1-63980-094-0

Kelsay Books
502 South 1040 East, A-119
American Fork, Utah 84003
Kelsaybooks.com

Debby, all day, every day.

Acknowledgments

I wish to acknowledge the publications in which the following poems have previously appeared.

Better Than Starbuck's: "Bookworm, A Fragment"
Shift, A Publication of MTSU Write: "Revelation"
Across the Margin: "Sonnet for Our Grandchildren," "Cataracts,"
"The Universe and All That Surrounds It"
Unlikely Stories Mark V: "His Own Devices"
Last Stanza Poetry Journal: "Equinoctial," "COVID Haiku"

These poems appear in my 2020 full-length collection from FutureCycle Press, *Where We're Going, Where We've Been:*

"Bookworm, a Fragment," "Revelation," "Sooner Than Later"

Contents

The Infernal *Now*

But our theory of the universe, called biocentrism, in which life and consciousness create the reality around them, has no space for death at all.
—*Biocentrism,* Bob Berman and Robert Lanza

I'm getting to the point where thoughts of death
Intrude more often on my days and nights
Than forty years ago, when drawing breath
Was thoughtless, pulsing on in gigabytes.
But now I hear my mind makes time and space
Irrelevant, and that I'll never die,
That every moment is a brand-new *place*
And time's flow is illusory. But why
My mind, awake or dreaming, has the power
To make that string of *nows* turn on a dime
And mark each non-existent passing hour
Seems more to me like reason without rhyme
Than living with a future and a past,
Where *now* means that each breath may be my last.

Love Token

For Debby

I gave my love a necklace with two rings,
Her name on one, the other bearing mine,
Connected by a heart of gold that sings
Our love's sweet song in its unique design.
Her elegance is understated, plain,
Her dresses always black, setting the ground
On which the rings, the heart, the silver chain,
Remind us of the way our lives are wound
Together, inextricably. And when
I see her simple pleasure in this gift,
I know I've chosen wisely, and again
Those rings entwine my heart, my spirits lift.
It's just a token, but it stands for love
Like fingers sliding warm into a glove.

Gone

It is the blight man was born for,
It is Margaret you mourn for.
—Gerard Manley Hopkins

Waiting in the car while my wife gets her COVID shot,
I listen to Joni sing "Carey, get out your cane,"
Her dulcimer like coins jangling into a tin pot,
Then the twanging of Stephen Stills, disguising pain
With lyrics and riffs that underpin his throat-catching
Whimsy in "Suite: Judy Blue Eyes." Then sweet Judy sings
"My Father" to rippling piano and her twelve-string
Gibson, back in the day of all those desperate flings,
Back when she and Joni, Stills, Crosby, and Nash were young.
Judy's album was *Who Knows Where the Time Goes?* It's gone,
All right, but the decades are nudged aside, and I'm sung
Back to the tacky apartment where I lived alone
On West Main Street, teaching sophomores how not to rhyme,
Playing my own songs absent my best friend's guitar licks
And stand-up bass. Because his new wife left him no time
For me, I'd backed off to give them peace, until at six
One night he'd shown up. "I took it as long as I could,"
He said, then moved in. He'd sit till the small hours and play
Joni's "Blue," while I tossed in bed, hoping his pain would
Pass, at least enough so we could face the coming day.
He took the bedroom another friend who'd lost his spouse
Had used; that friend, when my earnest efforts came undone,
Moved to a small crappy room in a crumbling frame house,
Where a few months later he left notes for everyone
He knew, including one for his landlady, taped up
Neatly to the front doorframe, instructing her to call
Police before entering. He sat in the bathtub
And shot himself, to leave no mess. At the funeral,
I learned his parents burned all of his notes like refuse.
Their anger blew my self-dramatizing guilt apart.

My other friend grieved as Joni sang away his blues,
And before too long he married his high-school sweetheart.
We played our own minor-league music in local bars.
The whole indulgent catalogue: the walking-away-
From-lovers playlist, Dylan, Cohen, Joni; and wars,
Vietnam and all the rest, hoping for a new day.
We took prank calls: “Do you have Prince Albert in a can?
Best let him out before he smothers.” Or, “Is John there?
What’s that? No John there? Do you shit in Dixie cups, man?”
And one from a married former student with red hair
Who asked what I’d say if she told me she was nearby,
Driving in nothing but high heels and a coat. For some
Strange reason I rebuffed her offer without a sigh,
Then hated myself for my unkindness: smug and dumb.
And our apartment actually saw two or three
Pals crawl off to sleep in the bath: too many tokes.
Another crashed with us long enough to have a key.
His snarling shaver woke us, giving rise to grim jokes
About Frank Zappa’s “Weasels Rip My Flesh.” Another
Time, Nelson Algren was a guest, and after reading
Something of mine, said, “More laughs. Otherwise, why bother?”
We’d met walking out on a Leslie Fiedler meeting,
Preferring the Billy Goat Tavern and its good cheer.
Nelson is gone now, with so many others. We wait
For our own turn. It may be near the point where we’re
No fun anymore. But we drive through the parking gate
Fortified by vaccine, my wife and I, while Joni sings
“Let’s not talk of fare-thee-wells now.” And though we may
mourn
For ourselves, like Margaret, we still love earthly things,
Still make music, look for the laughs, still glad we were born.

Bookworm, a Fragment

Bader's Drugstore on Kercheval and Gray,
Where I first saw books by Mickey Spillane
And the nude Marilyn issue of *Play-*
Boy, before puberty drove me insane,
While I still loved the Monteith Library
And the toasted paper smell of old books,
Hugh Lofting, Robert Heinlein, no Harry
Potter for decades yet to come, with nooks
Where I could sit amid the scent of wax
Polish at leather-topped tables, no cares
Except homesickness for Scotland, in *Pax*
Libris, then return to our place upstairs
From the greasy tavern, three books in hand,
A ten-year-old stranger in a strange land.

Revelation

You never know when revelation will visit.
The short block between our apartment
On the drab corner of Kercheval
And Springle, above the Blue Ribbon
Tavern, with its smells of beer and grease,
And Bader's Drugstore past the vacant
Lot at Kercheval and Gray, showed me
Something about myself one fall day.
My father had sent me out to buy—
Something—the *Detroit News,* aspirin,
Who knows what?—with a five-dollar bill
Tucked in my pocket. And I dawdled,
Thinking about birthdays. I was ten,
But I thought I couldn't wait to be
Nineteen, which seemed like the perfect age,
Because I knew it meant no more school,
Leaving me free to read any book
I wanted to.
But when I arrived
On the mosaic tile of Bader's entry,
I paused and checked my pocket,
Then all the others. Empty, of course.
I turned and retraced my steps, lingered
In the vacant lot between Bader's
And home. I spent at least half an hour
Searching amid grass, weeds, and gravel,
Knowing that the money was long-lost.
Strangely, I felt a sense of freedom,
Poised between loss and retribution.
I even found myself whistling,
Shifting from one foot to another,
Realizing that this was somehow
What the future held in store, as time

Would give and take at no one's bidding.
And after a while I turned for home
Slow-walking toward what might come next.

Laugh and Think

“What do you see in her?”
A friend asked long ago.
“She makes me laugh,” I said.
“Aha,” he came right back,
“But does she make you think?”
The moment called to mind
Past poetry readings,
Best served when they do both.
I dreamed last night about
A reading of my own:
A rectangular space
With me stood at one end
And a happy number
Of audience members
Filling the rectangle,
Not always a safe bet.
I led with “laugh and think,”
At which point the small crowd
Began to laugh and talk,
No doubt about thinking.
I stood there listening,
Counting all my own books
Piled on the sales table,
And looked ahead to wine
And little cubes of cheese.
I dreamt it made me laugh.

Sonnet for Our Grandchildren

We calculate the fits and starts of spring,
Feeling hopeful, though we see no sunshine,
Though climate change has not become a thing
The ignorant believe in; for in time
The seasons will assert themselves. Our hand
Wreaks havoc on the Earth; the Earth fights back.
And though we think its fate hangs by a strand,
It will erase our scarred and beaten track.
The sun will scorch with its indifferent brand,
And we'll inherit our deserved tomorrow,
Our trunkless legs stuck in the restless sand,
Unless we shift to beg, steal, or borrow
The means we see before us to keep blue
The arching sky and save the living dew.

His Own Devices

A rectangular fabric-covered behemoth, all edges and angles, the
color of sand
Laced with minerals, worn spots signaling the imminent
breakthrough of springs,
And marked by the residue of cat-vomit. The sofa calls to mind the
day
His next-door neighbor asked him to accompany her on a field trip
to a dredged
Canal in Dover to search for fossils amid the Mesozoic sludge and
shiny grit.
Mismatched furniture: two painted wooden chairs the color of
lizards;
A sun-catcher shaped like a bird hanging in the room's single
window;
A tiny television horned with antenna, complete with tinfoil to
improve reception;
A rickety brass floor lamp, shade askew; a frayed green hooked
rug
Matching the sofa's general air of overuse and obsolescence;
Stacks of nineteenth and early twentieth-century British novels;
A metal typing table with an antique typewriter that calls for
considerable
Hand-strength to operate the balky keys. The public-health
psychologist takes it all in.
They face each other on the mismatched chairs. Her hair in a bun,
professional jacket,
Skirt, blouse, feet crossed at the ankles, sensible low heels. Why is
she here?
"You're not sick," she says. He tells her he feels sick, that life
seems like something
He's living to fill time. And he does ask her why she's here, if not
to confirm that fact.

She says she never makes house calls, that she's only here because this will be
Their last meeting. "So you're dumping me," he says. "And my problems."
"Look at all these books," she says. She begins to pile them into a tower,
Then stops and looks at him. "You read these," she says. "You write. You're articulate,
Probably smarter than all my other clients. Maybe me, too." "So that means
You can't help me? Won't?" "It means you can help yourself." He tells her
That's a cliché of analysis and counseling. "You've just made my point," she says.
She tells him she got into public health counseling because private practice
Is full of clients like him. "You'd be a gold-mine," she says. "You'd talk and talk
And uncover more and more stuff to talk and talk about." She stacks more books,
Then smiles at him. "And I'd make money. I want to help clients who can't help themselves."
"So you're leaving me to my own devices." "Good way to put it," she says.
"Because you're good at constructing your own labyrinth. And when you're ready,
You'll find your own way out." She looks at the vomit-stained sofa. "And you have a cat."
"It died," he says with some satisfaction. Then, "Fine. Fine. How much do I owe you
For today?" She says she had a meeting on campus, then, "This is in the house—

And on the house." "Very funny," he says. She rises. "Goodbye,
then. Take care.
And remember—you're not sick." She leaves. He knocks over the
tower of books,
Then picks up *The History of Mr. Polly*. And gets back to his own
devices.

OCD at the Publix

The guy at the front of the checkout lane
In the Publix market on Longboat Key
Is not some doddering old fart, insane
Or demented. So far as we can see

We probably qualify more than he
As senior citizens. But in his brain
It's pretty clear to us something must be
Amiss, for he's unable to refrain

From inspecting each item in his cart
Before placing it like a blasting cap
On the conveyor, after which he'll start
The process again, making sure a gap

Remains between each item he must set
Down and the last, just like a picky child
Who'll insist that it's his right not to let
The potatoes, peas, and meatloaf be piled

Haphazard on the plate. He keeps an eye
On everything, but won't turn toward us,
As if his back could stop our nascent sigh.
His attention's on the unhurried fuss

Of the cashier and the bagger ringing
And bagging his purchases with scant care;
He looks uneasy, his radar pinging,
But makes no protest, just as we don't dare

Laugh aloud or voice exasperation
At this little pageant, one of many
Enacted here by the population
Of this barrier island on any

Given day. Elderly and affluent,
Self-absorbed, parking carts obstructively
In the aisles, looking as if they'd paid rent
To be there, musing narcissistically

In baffled contemplation of the shelves,
Or veering suddenly to block our way
For quirky reasons best known to themselves.
We slalom down the aisles each shopping day

With all the good grace we can muster; but
This guy, in cargo shorts and garish shirt,
Is something else, no ordinary nut.
His response to the cashier's smile is curt,

And, like a caveman at a cyclotron,
He works his credit card by fits and starts,
Then takes his groceries at last, moves on
To pageants starring cars and shopping carts.

The cashier and the bagger give us smiles,
Restrained and tactful, suggesting we're not
Part of the horde behind us in the aisles
Already puzzled by the goods they've bought.

But we all know we are, or will be soon,
So we say nothing, buy our stuff and go,
And pack our car out in the heat of noon,
Then leave our cart between the rails, just so.

Equinoctial

Inspired by Maryellen Hains, *Spring Equinox: Waxing Moon Spirit*

Joseph and his coat of many colors
Spring to mind in this season of rebirth,
As flowers appear amid the dolors
Of still-gray trees and slowly warming earth.
The trees, standing like brothers, know their green
Array may seem no more than fabric where
The favored flower's bright hues will be seen
As patterns stitched in an essential prayer.
But moving through the woods, surrounded by
The stir of growing things, the moon's clear beam
Waxing above us like an opened eye,
We know the flowers and trees share Joseph's dream:
The seasons turn, the equinoxes mark
How light would seem less dear without the dark.

The Universe and All That Surrounds It

With apologies to the creators of *Beyond the Fringe* (Peter Cook, Dudley Moore, Jonathan Miller, and Alan Bennett)

"Without consciousness, space and time are nothing."
—*Biocentrism*, Bob Berman and Robert Lanza

I know I'm biocentric, but I'm not
Convinced the universe has been apprised
That its complexity depends on me.
I don't know what's out there, beyond the stars
Or down among neutrinos, only seen
By other biocentered folk who seem
To work in ignorance of my vital
Role in the whole shebang. Why should I care
What they're up to, heed the whirl of planets,
Quarks, black holes, fish, ants, blowflies, all the rest
Of what I've dreamed up solipsistically?
It's certainly too much for me: I'm not
Aristotle, Archimedes, Newton,
Darwin, Einstein, Hawking, the gallery
Of rogues I've learned about, or concocted
From the stir of my own small nucleus.
Violet shifts, dopplering, all the strange
Attractors flesh is heir to. But I can't
Deny the universe goes on, with or
Without my help. At least that's how it seems
To me. I think we'll likely fall into
The sun. But I'll close on a cheerful note:
From my heart, I hope that will not happen.
And who's to say it's not all down to me?

Cataracts

1.

Drinking coffee at the Howard Johnson's
I overhear an old man behind me:
"I can't see. A cataract intervenes."
He says his eyepatch doesn't interfere
With sleeping, that he doesn't toss and turn
In bed, and that he always sleeps alone.
His woman companion commiserates.
He's grateful for her company, he says.
She says nothing. I watch them when they leave,
Note his tweed jacket, her pastel blue suit,
Hear her say, "Your fly is open, buster."
That happened almost forty years ago.

2.

Around that time, a friend said to me that
Our orchestra's Japanese-born maestro
Confided to him, "I have cataract."
My friend said, "That's too bad, Yoshi. Which eye?"
The maestro grinned. "Not in eye. Over there
In parking rot. Bland-new Eldolado."
Yoshi enjoyed playing his ethnic card.

3.

Now I'm probably older than the guy
In the Howard Johnson's, with cataracts
Parked in both of my eyes. My doctor's name
Sounds like an alias, though it isn't,
And he's teaching me about lens options,
Amblyopia, astigmatism,
And why they make for expensive choices.

4.

He removed my wife's cataracts last year.
I tell her my HoJo and maestro tales.
She says, "Forget Eldorados, buster.
You'll be fine. Dr. Doe will intervene
With a laser. And I'll make sure your fly
Is zipped up tightly. When it needs to be."

Sooner Than Later

Sooner than later he will cease to be,
He knows; the fragile network of his cells
Is closing checkpoints inexorably.
Though he's not quite prepared for tolling bells,

He knows the fragile network of his cells
Will work its algorithm and run down,
Spiraling inward like nautilus shells
To where "end" is no verb, but just a noun.

Will works its algorithm, too, runs down
As day flows inescapably to night
And "end" signifies nothing but a noun,
When what some call the soul takes its last flight.

As day flows inescapably to night
His little life will end its petty creep,
And what some call his soul will take its flight
Where atoms recombine but never sleep.

His little life will end its petty creep,
Shuffled and coiled relativistically
Where atoms recombine but never sleep,
The only way the cosmos sets us free.

Shuffled and coiled relativistically,
Sooner than later he will cease to be
The only way the cosmos sets us free:
Closing all checkpoints inexorably.

Covid Haiku

1.

Sidewalks lie empty
The streets quiet and breathless,
Trees and sky watching.

2.

City Hall is closed
And the skateboarders unmask,
Clacking on the steps.

3.

Sitting here at home
With the true love of my life.
The world in my arms.

4.

I give to myself
A fragment of my spent youth:
The moon and sixpence.

5.

The champagne is cold;
There's Dubliner cheddar, too.
And my love is near.

6.

Bumblebee appears
On our little balcony.
The world keeps turning.

September 11, One

The names go on and on, go on and on;
The bells ring out for all who graduate
From this class none of us foresaw at dawn
That bright September day, that bitter date
We recollect with shock and awe. Our grief,
Such as it is, can hardly touch the pain
Of those whose lives were ruined by a thief
In hiding half a world away. The plain
Truth is, though we assert ourselves and say
We'll never let such death and terror fall
Down on us once again, we know that day
Will come. So long as some of us can call
Up hatred in the name of what we love,
We know the birds of prey will rend the dove.

September 11, Two

My former student worked in Tower Two
At Morgan Stanley, just below the spot
Where that ill-fated airliner crashed through
The lives of everyone there on that fraught
Morning. The PA told them they should stay
Calm, help would be there soon. But they all knew
Before too long they had to get away,
To find an exit, had to stumble through
The smoke and chaos. So they disobeyed
That remote voice, descended floor by floor,
Passed firemen climbing upward, undismayed.
At last they reached ground level and the door
That led them to the streets, seeking relief,
And found instead this world of hope and grief.

Pantoum: Across the Universe

Raw energy is all there ever was,
Pulsing in waves across the universe,
Obedient to the ever-changing laws
Of quantum physics. Let it all disperse,

Pulsing in waves across the universe.
But where's the matter? Does it matter now,
When quantum physics lets it all disperse,
While spooky action stirs the cosmic row?

But where's the matter? Does it matter now,
When the observer makes the difference,
And spooky action stirs the cosmic row
In clear defiance of my common sense?

Does the observer make the difference?
Which is to say, am I the vital part,
In clear defiance of my common sense,
The horse that's left to trot behind the cart?

Perhaps I really am the vital part
As Einstein, Planck, and Heisenberg would say,
Trotting in theory behind the cart
That keeps the cosmic paradox in play.

Yes, Einstein, Planck, and Heisenberg would say,
Obedient to the ever-changing laws,
The cosmic paradox is still in play:
Raw energy is all there ever was.

The Center of It All

Quantum physics posits the observer
Is the still center of the whole shebang.
So here am I, calling up the fervor
Of the universe, all the *sturm und drang,*
Bemused though I am by the mess and stuff.
Plato tells me, and Einstein certainly,
Though Heisenberg would say that's not enough—
And Planck, and now biocentricity,
Again with me the center of it all,
Amid the voices of duplicity.
Now, as my summer eases into fall,
There's little hope for specificity.
But, if my other choice is endless night,
All I can say is, "Please, let there be light."

About The Author

Arnold Johnston lives in Kalamazoo and South Haven, MI. His poetry, fiction, non-fiction, and translations have appeared widely in literary journals and anthologies. His plays, and others written in collaboration with his wife, Deborah Ann Percy, have won over 300 productions and readings, as well as numerous awards and publications across the country and internationally; and they've written, co-written, edited, or translated over twenty books. Arnie's latest projects are a full-length poetry collection, *Where We're Going, Where We've Been* (FutureCycle Press, 2020); a novel, *Swept Away* (Atmosphere Press, 2021); and, with Debby, a children's book, *Mr. Robert Monkey Returns to New York* (Brandylane Publishers, 2021). His other books include two poetry chapbooks, *Sonnets: Signs and Portents* and *What the Earth Taught Us*; *The Witching Voice: A Play about Robert Burns*; *Of Earth and Darkness: The Novels of William Golding*; and *The Witching Voice: A Novel from the Life of Robert Burns*. His many accurate English versions of Jacques Brel's songs have appeared in numerous musical revues nationwide, and are also featured on his CD, *Jacques Brel: I'm Here!* From 2009-2012 Arnie and Debby were joint Arts and Entertainment columnists for the award-winning national quarterly journal *Phi Kappa Phi Forum*. A performer-singer, Arnie has played many solo concerts and over 100 roles on stage, screen, and radio; he has also done dialect coaching in a range of accents. He is a member of the Dramatists Guild, Poets & Writers, the Associated Writing Programs, and the American Literary Translators Association. He was chairman of the English Department (1997–2007) and taught for many years at Western Michigan University, where he co-founded the creative writing program and founded the playwriting program. He is now a full-time writer.

CPSIA information can be obtained
at www.ICGtesting.com
Printed in the USA
LVHW030052170522
718906LV00005B/964